NOTRE-DAME

ALSO BY KEN FOLLETT

The Modigliani Scandal
Paper Money
Eye of the Needle
Triple
The Key to Rebecca
The Man from St. Petersburg
On Wings of Eagles
Lie Down with Lions
The Pillars of the Earth
Night over Water
A Dangerous Fortune
A Place Called Freedom
The Third Twin
The Hammer of Eden
Code to Zero
Jackdaws
Hornet Flight
Whiteout
World Without End
Fall of Giants
Winter of the World
Edge of Eternity
A Column of Fire

NOTRE-DAME

A SHORT HISTORY OF THE MEANING OF CATHEDRALS

KEN FOLLETT

VIKING

VIKING
An imprint of Penguin Random House LLC
penguinrandomhouse.com

Page 67 constitutes an extension of this copyright page.

LIBRARY OF CONGRESS CATALOGING-IN-PUBLICATION DATA
Names: Follett, Ken, author.
Title: Notre-Dame : a short history of the meaning of cathedrals / Ken Follett.
Description: New York : Viking, [2019]
Identifiers: LCCN 2019024388 (print) | LCCN 2019024389 (ebook) | ISBN 9781984880253 (hardcover) | ISBN 9781984880260 (ebook)
Subjects: LCSH: Notre-Dame de Paris (Cathedral)| Cathedrals—France—Paris. | Paris (France)—Buildings, structures, etc.
Classification: LCC NA5550.N7 F65 2019 (print) | LCC NA5550.N7 (ebook) | DDC 726.60944/361—dc23
LC record available at https://lccn.loc.gov/2019024388
LC ebook record available at https://lccn.loc.gov/2019024389

Printed in the United States of America
1 3 5 7 9 10 8 6 4 2

Designed by Lauren Kolm and Meighan Cavanaugh

Translations from French
are by the author.

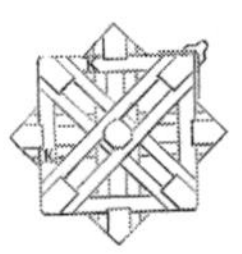

CONTENTS

It was one of those spring days that is so gentle and pretty that all Paris treats it like a Sunday, crowding the squares and the boulevards. During such days of clear skies, warmth and peace, there comes a supreme moment at which to appreciate the portal of Notre-Dame. It is when the sun, already sinking, shines almost directly on the cathedral. Its rays, more and more horizontal, slowly leave the pavement and climb the vertical façade to highlight the countless carvings against their shadows, until the great rose window, like the eye of the cyclops, is reddened as if by reflections from a furnace.

VICTOR HUGO,
The Hunchback of Notre Dame

Today, they weep for her in every language.

Paris-Match

CHAPTER ONE

2019

The voice on the phone was urgent. "I'm in Paris," it said. "Turn on your television!"

I was at home, in the kitchen, with Barbara, my wife. We had just finished supper. I had not drunk any wine, which turned out to be a good thing. I did not yet know it, but the evening was going to be a long one.

The voice on the phone belonged to an old friend. She has weathered many crises as a member of Parliament and a cabinet minister, and is completely unflappable, but she sounded shocked.

You know what we saw on the screen: the wonderful cathedral of Notre-Dame de Paris, one of the greatest achievements of European civilization, was on fire.

The scene dazed and disturbed us profoundly. I was on the verge of tears. Something priceless was dying in

front of our eyes. The feeling was bewildering, as if the earth was shaking.

I know the building well. One Christmas Barbara and I went to midnight Mass there. Thousands of people thronged the church. The dim lights cast deep shadows in the aisles, the carols echoed in the nave, and the vault high above us was cloaked in darkness. Most moving of all was the knowledge that our ancestors had been celebrating Christmas this way in this building for more than eight hundred years.

I had visited the church many other times. My earliest sight of it had been in 1966, on my first holiday outside the UK; although at the age of seventeen I'm afraid I was too interested in the girls in our group to pay serious attention to a cathedral. My last had been only four weeks earlier, when I had driven along the Left Bank and, as always, had drunk in the magnificent view of the twin towers and the flying buttresses.

As soon as I began to think rationally about what I was seeing on television I understood what was burning and how the fire was gathering force, but the journalists commenting did not—and why should they? They had not studied the construction of Gothic cathedrals. I had, in

doing research for *The Pillars of the Earth*, my novel about the building of a fictional medieval cathedral. A key scene in chapter four describes the old cathedral of Kingsbridge burning down, and I had asked myself: Exactly how does a great stone church catch fire?

I had climbed into the dusty spaces under the roofs of cathedrals including Canterbury and Florence. I had stood on the mighty beams that spanned the naves and looked at the rafters that supported the lead roof tiles. I had noticed the dried-up debris that often gathers in such places: old bits of wood and rope, sandwich wrappers left by maintenance workers, the knitted twigs of birds' nests, and the papery homes of wasps. I felt sure that the fire had started somewhere in the roof, probably when a dropped cigarette or a spark from an electrical fault ignited some litter, which in turn had set the timbers ablaze. And the damage resulting from that threatened to flatten the building.

I decided to share this thought with others, so I tweeted:

> The rafters consist of hundreds of tons of wood, old and very dry. When that burns the roof collapses, then the falling debris destroys the vaulted ceiling, which also falls and destroys the

> mighty stone pillars that are holding the whole thing up.

That turned out to be about right, except that I underestimated the strength of the pillars and the vaults, both of which were damaged but, happily, not completely obliterated.

Here's how the destruction of Kingsbridge Cathedral happened in *Pillars*, seen from the point of view of Prior Philip:

> A crashing sound made him look up. Immediately above him, an enormous timber was moving slowly sideways. It was going to fall on top of him. He dashed back into the south transept, where Cuthbert stood looking scared. A whole section of the roof, three triangles of beam-and-rafter plus the lead sheets nailed to them, was falling in. Philip and Cuthbert watched, transfixed, quite forgetting their own safety. The roof fell on one of the big round arches of the crossing. The enormous

> weight of the falling wood and lead cracked the stonework of the arch with a prolonged explosive sound like thunder. Everything happened slowly: the beams fell slowly, the arch broke up slowly, and the smashed masonry fell slowly through the air. More roof beams came free, and then, with a noise like a long slow peal of thunder, a whole section of the north wall of the chancel shuddered and slid sideways into the north transept. Philip was appalled. The sight of such a mighty building being destroyed was strangely shocking. It was like watching a mountain fall down or a river run dry: he had never really thought it could happen. He could hardly believe his eyes.

As night fell on April 15, 2019, the people of Paris came out into the streets, and the television cameras showed thousands of grief-stricken faces lit by the flames, some singing hymns, others just weeping as they watched their beloved cathedral burn. The tweet that got the most heartfelt response from my followers that night just said:

> Francais, francaises, nous partagons votre tristesse.
>
> Frenchmen, Frenchwomen, we share your sadness.

It should have been "nous partageons" with an *e* but no one minded.

There are people who understand more about medieval cathedrals than I do, but the journalists don't know their names. They know mine because of my books, and they know that *Pillars* is about a cathedral, so within a few minutes I started to get messages from the newsrooms. I spent that evening doing television, radio, and press interviews, explaining in English and French what was happening on the Île de la Cité.

At the same time as giving interviews I was watching.

The central spire, slender as an arrowhead and 300 feet high, was a possible starting point of the fire, and now it was blazing infernally. It was made of 500 tons of oak beams with a lead roof weighing 250 tons, and the burning wood rapidly became too weak to support the burden of all that lead. The most heart-stopping moment of the evening, for the grieving crowds on the streets and the

horrified millions watching television, came when the spire leaned sideways, snapped like a matchstick, and crashed through the flaming roof of the nave.

Notre-Dame had always seemed eternal, and the medieval builders certainly thought it would last until the Day of Judgment; but suddenly we saw that it could be destroyed. In the life of every boy there is a painful moment when he realizes that his father is not all-powerful and invulnerable. The old man has weaknesses, he may become ill, and one day he will die. The fall of the spire made me think of that moment.

It seemed that the nave was already a ruin. I thought I saw flames in one of the two towers, and I knew that if they fell the entire church would be destroyed.

President Macron, a radical modernizing leader who was in the middle of a bitter and violent battle with those who disliked his reforms, spoke to the cameras and became, for a time at least, the recognized leader of a united French nation. He impressed the world, and he brought tears to this Welshman's eyes when he said with firm confidence: "Nous rebattirons." We will rebuild.

At midnight I went to bed and set my alarm clock for

4:30 A.M., as my last phone call had been a request to appear on breakfast television early the following day.

I feared that the sun would rise on a smoking pile of rubble on the Île de la Cité, where Notre-Dame had so proudly stood. I was immensely heartened to see most of the walls still standing, as well as the great pair of square towers at the west end. It was not as bad as everyone had feared, and I drove to the television studio with a message of hope.

I spent Tuesday doing interviews, then on Wednesday I flew to Paris for a discussion on the TV program *La Grande Librairie* about the symbolism of cathedrals in literature and in life.

It never occurred to me to stay at home. Notre-Dame is too close to my heart. I'm not a religious believer, yet despite that I go to church. I love the architecture, the music, the words of the Bible, and the sense of sharing something profound with other people. I have long found deep spiritual peace in the great cathedrals, as do many millions of people, believers and nonbelievers alike. And I have another reason to feel grateful for the cathedrals: my love of them inspired the novel that is certainly my most popular book and probably my best.

President Macron said Notre-Dame would be rebuilt in five years. One of the French newspapers responded with a headline that translates: MACRON BELIEVES IN MIRACLES. But French attachment to Notre-Dame is profound. It has been the stage for some of the key events in French history. Every road sign that tells you how far you are from Paris measures the distance to Kilometer Zero, a bronze star embedded in the pavement in front of Notre-Dame. The great bell called Emmanuel, in the south tower, can be heard all over the city when it rings its deep F sharp for joy or sorrow, the end of war or a tragedy, such as 9/11.

Besides, it is always unwise to underestimate the French. If anyone can do it, they can.

Before I flew home from Paris, my French publisher asked me if I would think about writing something new about my love of Notre-Dame, in the light of the terrible event of April 15. Profits from the book would go to the rebuilding fund, and so would my royalties. "Yes," I said. "I'll start tomorrow."

This is what I wrote.

CHAPTER TWO

1163

The cathedral of Notre-Dame was too small in 1163. The population of Paris was growing. On the right bank of the river, commerce was surging to levels unknown in the rest of medieval Europe; and on the left bank the university was attracting students from many countries. Between the two, on an island in the river, stood the cathedral, and Bishop Maurice de Sully felt it should be bigger.

And there was something else. The existing building was in the round-arched style we call Romanesque, but there was an exciting new architectural movement that used pointed arches, letting more light into the building; a look now called Gothic. This style had been pioneered only six miles from Notre-Dame, at the abbey church of

St.-Denis—burial place of the French kings—which had brilliantly combined several technical and visual innovations: as well as the pointed arch it featured piers of clustered shafts sprouting ribs up into a high vault that was lighter in weight; a semicircular walkway at the east end to keep pilgrims moving past the relics of St. Denis; and, outside, graceful flying buttresses that facilitated larger windows and made the massive church look as if it were about to take flight.

Sully must have seen the new church of St.-Denis and become enamored of it. No doubt it made Notre-Dame look old-fashioned. Perhaps he was even a little jealous of Abbot Suger at St.-Denis, who had encouraged two successive master masons to experiment boldly, with triumphantly successful results. So Sully ordered his cathedral to be knocked down and replaced by a Gothic church.

Let me pause. All the above sounds straightforward, but in fact it is astonishing. The cathedral of Notre-Dame de Paris, and most of the great Gothic churches that are still the most beautiful buildings in the cities of Europe, were erected in the Middle Ages, a time marked by violence, famine, and plague.

The construction of a cathedral was a huge enterprise

lasting decades. Chartres Cathedral was built in twenty-six years, and Salisbury in thirty-eight years, but they were unusually quick. Notre-Dame de Paris took almost one hundred years, and improvements continued after that.

It required hundreds of workers, and it cost a fortune. The modern equivalent would be a moon shot.

That huge building was erected by people who lived in wooden huts with straw roofs, people who slept on the floor because only the rich had beds. The towers are 223 feet high, yet the builders did not have the mathematics to calculate the stresses in such structures. They proceeded by trial and error, and they made mistakes. Sometimes their work collapsed: Beauvais Cathedral fell down twice.

We take for granted our ability to go to a hardware store to buy a perfectly balanced hammer with a steel head for a few dollars, but the tools of the cathedral builders were crude, and steel was so expensive that it was used very sparingly, often for only the tip of a blade.

Notre-Dame and all cathedrals were richly decorated, yet the builders wore simple homespun tunics. The cathedral owned gold and silver plates and chalices, crucifixes and candlesticks, while the congregation drank from wooden cups and burned smoky rush lights.

How did this happen? How did such majestic beauty arise out of the violence and filth of the Middle Ages?

The first part of the answer is something almost always left out of any history of cathedrals: the weather.

The years 950 to 1250 are known to climatologists as the medieval climatic anomaly. For three hundred years the weather in the North Atlantic region was better than usual. The evidence comes from tree rings, ice cores, and lake deposits, all of which tell us about long-term weather changes in the past. There were still occasional years of bad harvests and famine, but on average the temperature was higher. Warm weather meant more crops and wealthier people. And so Europe emerged from the long depression known as the Dark Ages.

Whenever human beings manage to produce more than they need to survive, someone comes along to take the surplus away from them. In medieval Europe there were two such groups, the aristocracy and the church. The noblemen fought wars and, between battles, went hunting to maintain their equestrian skills and their bloodthirsty spirit. The church built cathedrals. Bishop Sully had money for his project—or, at least, to begin it.

He hired a master builder, someone whose name we

don't know, and the master produced a design. But this was not drawn on paper. The art of making paper was new to Europe in the twelfth century and the product was an expensive luxury. Books such as the Bible were written on parchment, which is a fine leather, also expensive.

Masons drew their designs on a tracing floor. Mortar was spread on the ground and allowed to harden, then the plans were drawn with a sharply pointed iron instrument such as a nail. At first the scratch lines were white, but they faded over time, allowing new designs to be drawn on top of the old. Some tracing floors have survived, and I have studied them at York Minster and Wells Cathedral.

There would have been long discussions between Bishop Sully and his master mason, as the bishop explained what he wanted—a modern church filled with light—and the mason figured out how the dream could be achieved. Even so, both knew that as building progressed the design would be modified over the years by new ideas and new people.

The height of the projected building might have been an important subject of these meetings. According to the historian Jean Gimpel, in *The Cathedral Builders*, every town wanted to have the highest church:

> The young medieval society represented by the bourgeoisie, in its enthusiasm, was seized by the "world record" fad, and sent the naves soaring towards the sky.

The nave of Notre-Dame would be 108 feet high—the tallest in the world (though not for long: it was overtaken by Chartres a few years later).

Meanwhile, the old cathedral was coming down. Its materials were not discarded, though. The best of the stones were stacked on the site to form the foundations of the new church. Even the debris was kept, because the wall of a medieval cathedral is a sandwich of two skins of dressed stone with a filling of rubble.

More stone was ordered. This was not the famous creamy-gray "Paris stone," technically Lutetian limestone, used for the Louvre, the Invalides, the Hollywood homes of movie millionaires, and for Giorgio Armani's stores all over the world today. That was not discovered until the seventeenth century and comes from quarries twenty-five miles north of Paris in the Department of the Oise. In the Middle Ages the cost of transporting stone could be prohibitive. Notre-Dame used limestone from numerous

quarries close at hand, just outside the boundaries of Paris.

The master would have separated stones of different characteristics: harder ones were used for structural supports that needed to bear enormous weights; softer, more easily carved stones were kept for non-load-bearing decorative details.

Once the design was finalized, the builders needed an agreed system of measurement. A yard, a pound, and a gallon were not the same everywhere. Each building site had its own yardstick, an iron rod that told every worker exactly how long a yard should be.

By this time the city of Paris must have had its own standard measures, on display near the quayside on the right bank of the Seine. Paris was already a commercial city, probably the largest in Europe, and it was important to such places that a yard of cloth, a pound of silver, or a gallon of wine should be the same size in every shop in town so that customers knew what they were buying. (No doubt there were also merchants who complained about too much government regulation!) So it's likely that the master mason of Notre-Dame made his yardstick the same as that of the merchants of Paris.

With a design on the tracing floor and a yardstick in his hand the master mason laid out the shape of the cathedral on the ground where the old church had stood, and building could begin.

Suddenly Paris needed more craftsmen and laborers, especially masons, carpenters, and mortar makers. There were some residents in the city, but not enough for this ambitious new project. However, cathedral builders were nomads, traveling from city to city throughout Europe in search of work (and, as they did so, spreading technical innovations and new styles). As word got around that Paris was building a cathedral, they began to come in from the provinces and beyond, from Italy and the Netherlands and England.

There were women as well as men. Jean Gimpel read the thirteenth-century tax register of the municipality of Paris and found many female names on the list of craftspeople who paid taxes. Gimpel was the first historian to note the role of women in building our great cathedrals. The idea that women are too weak for this kind of work is nonsense, but it might be true that the structure of the male arm is better designed for hammering action. In any event, women were plasterers and mortar makers more

often than hammer-and-chisel masons. They frequently worked as part of a family team, husband and wife and older children, and it is easy to imagine the man cutting stone, the woman making mortar, and the teenagers fetching and carrying sand, lime, and water.

Most cathedrals were built by an international effort. The designer of England's premier cathedral, Canterbury, was a Frenchman, Guillaume De Sens. Men and women of different nations worked side by side on these building sites, and foreigners are right to see Notre-Dame as their heritage as well as that of the French nation.

The work was dangerous. Once the wall grew taller than the mason, he had to work on a platform, and as the wall rose higher, so did the platform. Medieval scaffolding was a precarious construction of branches tied together with rope, and medieval people drank a great deal of ale. Guillaume De Sens fell off the scaffolding at Canterbury, and he was one of many.

The builders of Notre-Dame started at the east end, as usual. There was a practical reason for this. As soon as the choir was finished, the priests could start holding services there while the rest of the church was going up.

But the construction of Notre-Dame went badly. We

don't know why, though money was the commonest cause of building delays. (Other causes might include strikes, disruption of supplies, and collapses.) When funds ran low, artisans would be laid off, and the work would proceed slowly until more money came in. It was twenty-six years before the high altar was consecrated.

Even then the choir was not finished, because cracks appeared in the stones. The master mason decided that the vault was too heavy. However, the solution was a happy one: to reinforce the walls, he added the elegant flying buttresses that today make the view from the east so enchanting, like a flock of birds rising into the air.

From then on the work went even more slowly. While Chartres Cathedral was rising fast only fifty miles away, Notre-Dame went on in fits and starts.

New styles emerged. The rose windows, perhaps the best-loved features of Notre-Dame, were a late addition, begun in the 1240s by the first mason whose name we know, Jean de Chelles. The stained glass was made late in the building process, when the structure was firmly established.

The twin towers were in place by 1250. Probably the last phase was the casting of the bells. As these were

well-nigh impossible to transport over any distance they were cast on site, and the builders of Notre-Dame probably made a bell pit near the base of the west front so that the finished article could be hauled up directly into the tower.

The cathedral was more or less built by 1260. But Bishop Sully had died in 1196. He never saw his great cathedral finished.

CHAPTER THREE

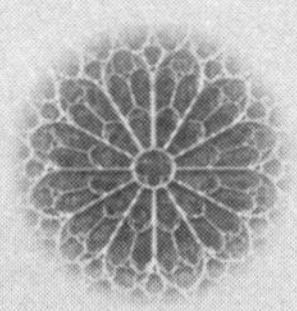

1831

At the age of twenty-nine Victor Hugo was a famous poet. As a young man he had written two novels but they had not been very successful and few people read them today. However, his plays had caused a stir. *Marion de Lorme* was suppressed by the censor and *Hernani* was so scandalous that it provoked rioting in the theater of the Comédie Française.

Hugo represented one side in a literary controversy, the conflict between Classicists and Romantics. It's a dispute that seems, to modern readers, as pointless as the medieval argument about how many angels can dance on the head of a pin; but in nineteenth-century Paris it got intellectuals sufficiently riled up to punch one another. Hugo was seen as a representative of the Romantics.

Paradoxically, the young poet was a conservative in politics. Born in the aftermath of the French Revolution, he wanted to see the French monarchy restored. The revolutionaries had rejected all religion and had turned Notre-Dame into a "Temple of Reason"; and they had venerated the Goddess of Reason, often depicted as a woman revealingly draped in the red, white, and blue colors of the French flag; but young Hugo believed in the authority of the Catholic Church. He even founded a magazine called *The Literary Conservative*.

However, he changed. He wrote in his diary: "In the last ten years my former royalist and Catholic conviction of 1820 has crumbled piece by piece before age and experience." He produced a short semifictional work called *The Last Days of a Condemned Man*, a strikingly compassionate account of the final hours of a man condemned to death, based on a real-life murderer. He was beginning to see French society as sometimes harsh and cruel, and his imagination was more and more occupied by the despised: prisoners, orphans, cripples, beggars, and murderers. And like every novelist he burned to transform his obsessions into stories. He was moving rapidly toward the social

criticism that thirty years later would produce his masterpiece, *Les Misérables.*

He had long ago taken an advance from a publisher for a historical novel set in Paris, and he had done a lot of research; but he kept postponing the actual writing. His publisher was at first forgiving, as they usually are, but eventually became more insistent, as they usually do.

On September 1, 1830, he sat down to write chapter one. His wife recalled: "He bought himself a bottle of ink and a huge grey knitted shawl, which covered him from head to foot; locked away his formal clothes, so that he would not be tempted to go out; and entered his novel as if it were a prison." (Writers are often swathed in wool, by the way; we sit still all day, so we get cold.)

By the middle of January 1831 the book was, astonishingly, finished. He had written something like 180,000 words in four and a half months. And it was very, very good.

Set in the year 1482, it had the same name as the cathedral, *Notre-Dame de Paris*. The heroine is Esmerelda, a beautiful gypsy girl who dances in the street for pennies. The three other major characters are men who fall in love

with her: the penniless student Pierre Gringoire, the haughty archdeacon Claude Frollo, and the deformed bell ringer Quasimodo.

It got poor reviews but the public loved it, and it was quickly translated into other languages. The English edition was called *The Hunchback of Notre-Dame*, a title at once more vulgar and more alluring. And Hugo became world famous.

Hugo admired the work of Walter Scott, often said to be the inventor of the historical novel; but he wrote, in a review of *Quentin Durward*, that the genre could do more. He did not say that he could write better than Scott, but he surely thought it, and to my mind he was right. He would never produce a sentence as constipated as this, picked almost at random from Scott's *Waverley*:

> The drawing-room of Flora Mac-Ivor was furnished in the plainest and most simple manner; for at Glennaquioich every other sort of expenditure was retrenched as much as possible, for the purpose of maintaining, in its full dignity, the hospitality of the chieftain,

> and retaining and multiplying the number of
> his dependents and adherents.

Hugo wanted to write more like Homer, author of the central works of Greek literature *The Odyssey* and *The Iliad*. He created works of color and grandeur and passion that, to my mind, make Walter Scott pale by comparison.

Notre-Dame de Paris takes the reader into the criminal underworld, whose filth and violence Hugo describes with a mixture of disgust and relish that cannot help but remind us of his contemporary Charles Dickens. This fascination with low life was hugely successful among readers, and it spawned imitators. Eugène Sue's vividly sensational *The Mysteries of Paris* was more popular than Hugo's novel in the short term. Sue's work was published in 150 installments on the front page of the newspaper *Le Journal des Débats*. It captured the imagination of the nation, being read aloud in factories and offices, cafés and bars. However, it lacked the timeless distinction of Hugo's work and is hardly ever read today.

Many of Hugo's characters are preposterously larger than life, teetering dangerously on the cliff edge of absurdity.

As well as those already mentioned we meet the vicious king of the thieves, Clopin Trouillefou; the hermit Sister Gudule, who lives walled up in self-imprisonment for years; the judge Florian Barbedienne, who issues random verdicts because he is stone deaf and has no idea what is going on in his court; and the hopelessly dissolute Jehan Frollo.

In the twenty-first century we believe that people who are different from the average should not be defined by their difference, but seen in the round. Novelists have never worked that way: rather, they use differences to express personality. Shylock and Fagin are defined by their Jewishness; Captain Hook and Blind Pugh are defined by their disability; and the list of characters defined by their sexual orientation is very long—E. M. Forster's Maurice, Patricia Highsmith's Carol, George R. R. Martin's Renly Baratheon, Ian Fleming's Pussy Galore, and many more.

Quasimodo is defined by his ugliness.

> In fact he was wicked because he was feral,
> and he was feral because he was ugly.

In order to tell his highly colored tale of angry confrontations and incessant crises Hugo developed a

style of extraordinary vividness and power, muscular enough to carry the weight of all that melodrama. The greatest and most popular novelists, from Jane Austen to Ian Fleming, have often created highly individual prose tailored to suit the material of their stories.

The quality of Hugo's writing is well illustrated by a passage in which he imagines, with spooky prescience, a fire at Notre-Dame:

> All eyes were lifted to the heights of the church. What they saw was extraordinary. At the top of the highest gallery, above the rose window, a tall flame rose between the two bell towers with a tornado of sparks, a tall flame reckless and angry, from time to time shredded into the smoke by the wind. Below this flame, below the dark balustrade with its glowing leaves, two gutters vomited relentlessly through monster mouths a hard rain that gleamed silver against the dark façade. As they approached the ground, the two jets of liquid lead widened into multiple streamlets, like the spray from the thousand holes of a watering-can. Above

> the flame the vast towers, each harsh and sharply carved, one all black, the other all red, seemed even bigger because of the immense shadow they cast up to the sky. The innumerable sculptures of devils and dragons took on a dismal look. The restless brightness of the flames made them seem to fidget. There were laughing vipers, yapping gargoyles, salamanders fanning the fire with their breath, and monsters that sneezed in the smoke.

No one had ever written like this before.

The novel that Notre-Dame inspired Hugo to write has been made into at least thirteen films, five television series, five plays, fifteen stage musicals, five ballets, two BBC radio serials, and a video game, according to Wikipedia. There may be many more versions. Probably the most distinguished film is the 1939 black-and-white version starring Charles Laughton as Quasimodo. I remember seeing it as a boy, on someone's tiny 1960s television set, and being scared stiff.

Hugo's novel swept the world, but it did more.

Nineteenth-century novelists felt free to stop the story and insert a long passage of barely relevant description

Maurice de Sully,
bishop of Paris,
ordered the building
of a new cathedral
in the year 1163.

Notre-Dame after completion.

Liberty Leading the People by Eugène Delacroix
is a painting celebrating revolution in France.

Eugène Viollet-le-Duc was commissioned to renovate the cathedral after years of damage and neglect during the revolutionary period in France.

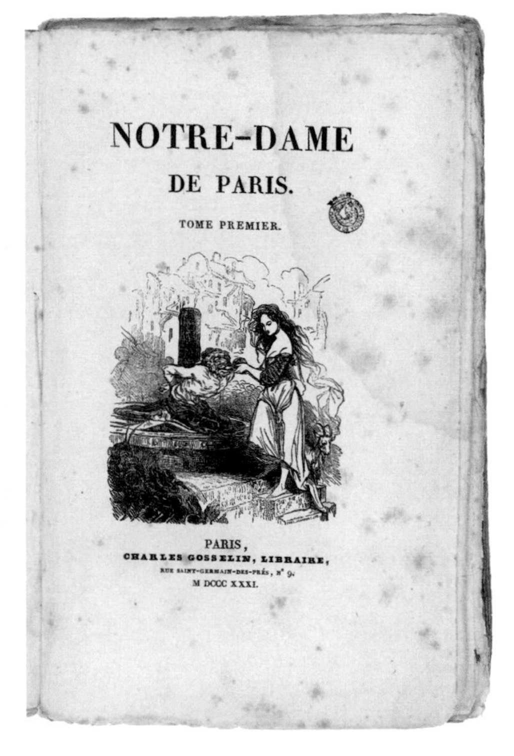

NOTRE-DAME
DE PARIS.
TOME PREMIER.

PARIS,
CHARLES GOSSELIN, LIBRAIRE,
RUE SAINT-GERMAIN-DES-PRÉS, N° 9.
M DCCC XXXI.

Victor Hugo's hugely popular novel was inspired by the cathedral.

Viollet-le-Duc made drawings of many features of the cathedral that had to be repaired or replaced. This sketch is owned by the author.

Viollet-le-Duc also made use of the brand new invention of photography.
He commissioned this daguerreotype of the west front.

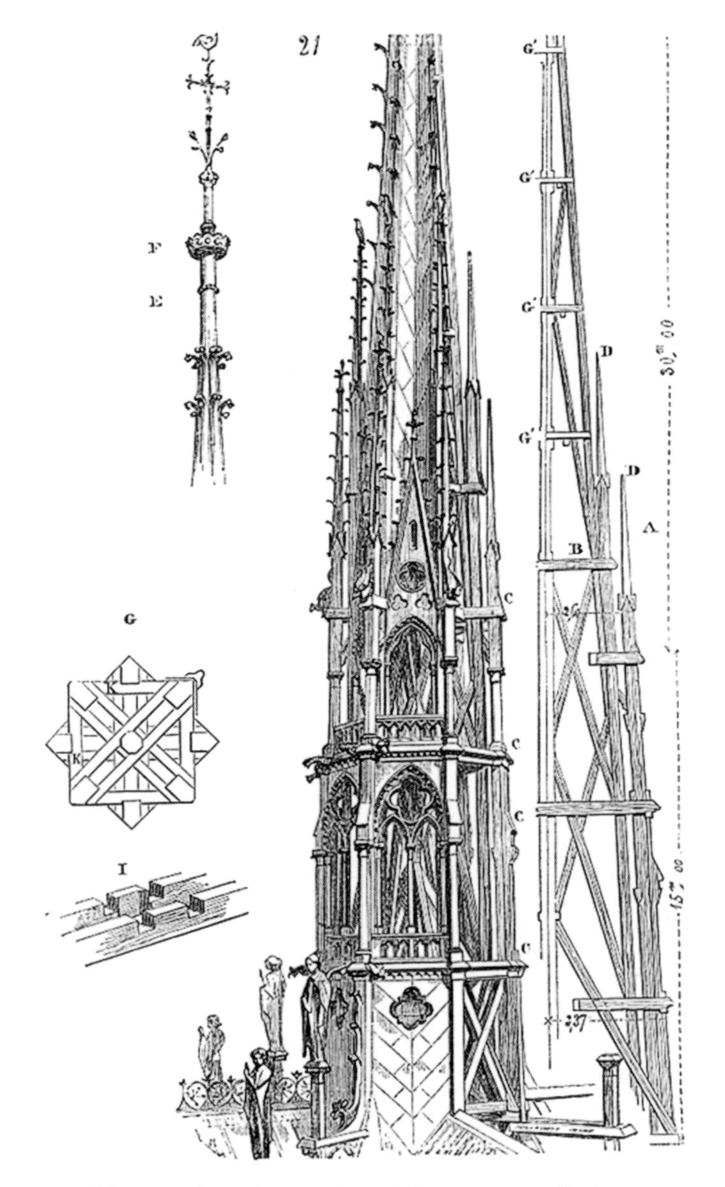

The spire, shown here in a beautiful drawing by Viollet-le-Duc, collapsed tragically during the fire of April 15, 2019.

The spire, a nineteenth-century addition, was constructed in about 1860.

After restoration, the cathedral was reconsecrated in 1864.

On August 26, 1944, the day after Paris was liberated, General Charles de Gaulle led a victory march along the Champs Élysées and took part in a service of thanksgiving in Notre-Dame.

In June 2019, the author was privileged to inspect the damaged cathedral and interview the architect in charge of restoration, Philippe Villeneuve.

and opinion. There are many in *Notre-Dame de Paris*, but the most passionate are about the cathedral.

At the beginning of Book Three Hugo wrote:

> The church of Notre-Dame de Paris is still today a majestic and sublime building. But, beautifully though it has aged, we must sigh, and we must feel outraged at the degradation and mutilation that time and men have inflicted on this awesome monument. . . .

Hugo was angry about this. Notre-Dame had been much abused during the French Revolution and afterward. Its statuary had been damaged and its nave had been used as a grain store.

Both Hugo's eulogistic descriptions of the beauty of Notre-Dame and his outraged protests about its dereliction moved the readers of his book. A worldwide bestseller, it attracted tourists and pilgrims to the cathedral, and the half-ruined building they saw shamed the city of Paris. His indignation spread to others. The government decided to do something.

A competition was held to choose the expert who

would supervise the renovation of the cathedral. Two young architects collaborated on the winning proposal. One of them died suddenly, but the other went on to do the work. His name was Eugène Viollet-le-Duc.

He was thirty when he won the job, and he would be fifty before it was finished.

CHAPTER FOUR

1844

Viollet-le-Duc came from a family steeped in French high culture. His grandfather was an architect; his uncle was a painter who studied under the great Jacques-Louis David; and his father was governor of the royal residences.

All his adult life Viollet-le-Duc visited medieval buildings, drew them beautifully, and theorized about architecture. His writings and drawings are collected in the *Encyclopédie Médiévale*, a massive volume full of detail and insight. With his mentor Prosper Mérimée he worked on the restoration of numerous buildings, including Sainte-Chapelle, a royal church that had been built around the same time as Notre-Dame on the Île de la Cité.

He loved his job. Looking back, he said: "Work was the best part of our day." He was obsessed with medieval

architecture, and he adored the cathedral of Notre-Dame de Paris. There was no one in the world better qualified to renovate Notre-Dame.

He began by meticulously making a color-coded map showing the location and type of every stone in the areas needing repair.

Laborers began to remove the damaged stones. The statues over the west portals had been beheaded during the revolution, and more than sixty had to be replaced. Other decorative features such as gargoyles and chimeras had been smashed.

As they were taken down Viollet-le-Duc made drawings of what was left, displaying the painstaking draftsmanship that must have been a reflection of his innermost character. I am the proud owner of one of those drawings. It shows a corbel, which is a support for a shaft, carved as the head of an imaginary monster.

He also exploited the new technology of photography to make daguerreotypes.

Where there was nothing left but an empty space he used drawings and photographs from other medieval cathedrals to design substitutes. He drew Gothic windows to replace the medieval stained glass broken in the revolution.

Viollet-le-Duc replaced those of the bells that had been melted down for cannons in the revolution. (The great Emmanuel had somehow survived.) In the north tower he put a new, stronger timber support structure; and as I watched with horrified eyes on April 15, I thought I saw fire inside that tower. Later reports said those flames had been extinguished just in time by firefighters who had bravely ascended the tower at the risk of their lives.

Viollet-le-Duc put together a team of skilled masons, carpenters, sculptors, and glaziers to repair or reproduce the impaired stonework.

His aim was to restore the church to its original look, but he was not sufficiently meticulous to satisfy the most conservative critics. His gargoyles were not very medieval, they complained, and the chimeras—monstrous animals—that he created to decorate the roof were not like anything else in the church. The ambulatory and the chapels that radiate from it were said to be overdecorated, an unusual fault to find with a Gothic cathedral, a bit like saying that a party frock is too pretty. The restored south rose window has some of the figures in the wrong order, apparently.

Worst of all, the new spire was positively modern.

The medieval cathedral had had a central tower with a spire. Victor Hugo described it as "this charming little bell-tower," although he never saw it: it was dismantled before he was born. He wrote angrily of the architect who removed it, but in all likelihood it had become weak and was in danger of being blown down.

As far as I know there is no reliable description of the original tower, just two sketches. In any event Viollet-le-Duc made no attempt to imitate a medieval tower in his design for the replacement, and this is the loudest complaint of his critics. Instead, he modeled the new spire on a similar one recently added to the cathedral at Orléans. At its base were images of three disciples, and it was said that the face of St. Thomas staring up at the spire looked remarkably like that of Viollet-le-Duc himself.

The criticism did him no harm. He spent the rest of his life as the leading expert in his field. He was consulted on the repair and renovation of dozens of buildings, and he wrote copiously on theories of architecture. He seemed to have no end of energy. In his sixties he was elected to the Paris city council. He died at the age of sixty-five after spending the summer hiking in the Alps.

CHAPTER FIVE

1944

The chapel of St. Joseph is halfway along the south side of the nave. In 1944 it contained a statue of Joseph holding the baby Jesus. On August 26, the morning after Paris was liberated, Mass was said in the chapel in English by a bespectacled American priest, Father Leonard Fries, wearing borrowed French robes.

The chapel is less than 130 square feet and contained an altar as well as the statue, but the service was attended by 300 men, mostly of the U.S. Army 12th Infantry Regiment, all carrying carbines or full-length rifles and holding their helmets in their hands. They overflowed into the aisle and the nave of the great cathedral. As the sun rose into a cloudless sky and shone through the stained glass of the east end, some of the men who had freed Paris knelt

to remember the comrades they had left behind on the beaches of Normandy.

It was the first service that day, but later there would be another, much bigger. The radio that morning announced that General de Gaulle would lead a victory march along the Champs-Élysées at 2:00 P.M. and attend a thanksgiving service of Te Deum at 4:30 in the cathedral of Notre-Dame.

De Gaulle had been head of the provisional French government in exile and was determined to become the new leader of the liberated country, but his right to do so was debatable. He was at odds with the Resistance leaders, who had stayed to fight the Germans here in France while he was living at the Connaught Hotel in London. Now he was determined to position himself as de facto president. When Napoleon crowned himself emperor of the French on December 2, 1804, he did it at Notre-Dame. And de Gaulle knew that if he was going to make himself look like France's new ruler he needed to do it in Notre-Dame.

His unilateral announcement of a victory parade infuriated the Allies. Paris was not yet secure. There were still German soldiers in the city. General Leonard Gerow had ordered the French 2nd Armored Division to guard

the northeast suburbs against a possible German counter-attack, but he was told that de Gaulle, ignoring the chain of command, had commandeered the division for his parade.

De Gaulle outmaneuvered the Resistance and the Allied command, and he got his parade.

De Gaulle had also failed to ask anyone's permission to hold a service in the cathedral, but Cardinal Emmanuel Suhard, the archbishop of Paris, was merely the next authority to crumble before the irresistible force of de Gaulle's will.

At about the same time General Alfred Jodl in Germany placed a call to Army Group B at Margival in France and asked for Field Marshal Walter Model. The field marshal was not in the underground bunker, so Jodl spoke to General Hans Speidel. Repeating Hitler's personal instructions, Jodl ordered a massive V-1 bomb attack on Paris that night.

Speidel never passed the message on. A week later he was arrested by the Gestapo.

De Gaulle was late for the parade, but no one cared. He arrived at ten past three at the Arc de Triomphe. Acting as if he was already the head of state, he lit the

eternal flame and laid a wreath of red gladiolus on the Tomb of the Unknown Soldier. Then he turned and looked along the Champs Élysées.

Thousands of Parisians, dozens of journalists, and several film cameras were waiting for him. The spectators crowded the sidewalks of the broad boulevard, climbed the chestnut trees, leaned from windows and balconies, and even stood on the rooftops, waving flags and banners, all the way to the Obelisk.

A group of several hundred men and women broke through the crowd onto the road dressed in seventeenth-century costume, the women draped in red, white, and blue, and topless like the goddess in Delacroix's painting. Having made their point, whatever it was, they vanished again.

Before ordering the parade to move off, de Gaulle gave one more vital instruction: he told his entourage that they should all take care to remain at least one step behind him for the entire march.

Then, unmistakably the hero of the hour, he set off at the head of the procession.

De Gaulle reached the Place de la Concorde and was approaching an open-top Hotchkiss—a French-made

luxury car—that stood waiting to take him onward to Notre-Dame when shots were heard.

Thousands of spectators threw themselves flat or took cover behind the vehicles of the 2nd Armored Division. Stretcher bearers dressed in white ran into the crowd to see to the casualties.

No one knew who was firing. It was probably German snipers left behind in the city, but it might have been Resistance fighters angry that they were not leading the parade, or Communists opposed to de Gaulle's takeover.

De Gaulle was impervious. He did not duck or take cover or even pause in his stately progress. He might easily have been killed, and clearly he was prepared to risk death at this crucial moment in his career and in the history of France. He climbed into the open car, ordered the driver on, and sat waving to the crowds, unprotected, all the way to the Île de la Cité.

It was a masterpiece of political theater. Fearless, dignified, and strong-willed—and six feet five inches tall—he appeared exactly the man to drive France's postwar recovery. Film and photographs of his performance were all over the world within hours.

As he arrived in front of the Cathedral of Notre-Dame,

more shots rang out. Snipers had gotten into the north tower.

In reply, the French soldiers of the 2nd Armored raked the tower and the rooftop with fire, sending fragments of limestone flying off the statues so carefully restored by Viollet-le-Duc. De Gaulle, unheeding, stepped out of his car and received a bouquet—red, white, and blue flowers—from a scared but brave little girl. Then he entered by the Portal of the Last Judgment.

Most of the congregation was on the floor as gunfire rang out in the nave. "One could see more bottoms than faces," an observer said later. De Gaulle did not change his pace. His seat was 190 feet away down the nave, and he walked the entire distance with a majestically slow step.

As he reached his place General Pierre Koenig, commander of the French Forces of the Interior, bellowed at the congregation: "Stand up!"

The priest sang the opening words of the Magnificat: "My soul magnifies the Lord."

And then the nave echoed with the sound of the people of Paris singing.

CHAPTER SIX

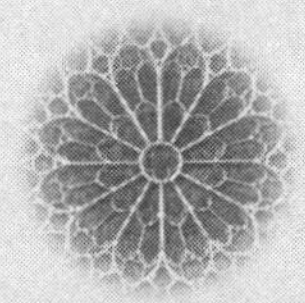

1989

Every year, millions of people visit Notre-Dame and other cathedrals. They are the oldest buildings in northwest Europe. There are even more ancient buildings elsewhere—Roman ruins, Greek temples, the Egyptian pyramids—but I think our cathedrals are the oldest still used for their original purpose.

The cathedrals have always attracted tourists. Today's visitors come not just from Europe but from very different cultures, Japan and the United States and India. When all these visitors look at our cathedrals, what do they think?

We often catch our first glimpse from a distance. As at Chartres, the towers of the church appear over the horizon when we are still miles away. The medieval visitor must have been awestruck by the sight, as he was meant to be.

Our next reaction, as we come closer, is often

confusion. It seems too complicated to understand. It's a bit like the first time you hear a Beethoven symphony. There are so many melodies, rhythms, instruments, and harmonies that at first you can't grasp how they are linked and interrelated. It is hard to see the logic. A cathedral, like a symphony, has a coherent plan, its windows and arches form rhythms, its decorations have themes and tell stories, but the whole thing is so rich that at first it overwhelms us.

When we step inside, this changes. Most people experience a sense of tranquility. The cool air, the ancient stones, the regular repetitions of the architecture, and the way the entire building seems to reach toward heaven, all work together to soothe the human soul.

The first thing most of us do inside the cathedral is buy a guidebook. This may tell us that the site was a place of worship before Christianity was invented. Notre-Dame was the location of a temple to the Roman god Jupiter.

Often we learn that the church was not built all at once, the way a modern skyscraper or shopping mall would be. We may find that the early Christians had a wooden church, of which nothing now remains. Notre-Dame is the fifth church built on the site. Often the

building of the current church began when the old one burned down. Sometimes the chapter ran out of money, and work halted for a hundred years.

At the end of a visit to a cathedral, if we're lucky, we no longer feel confused. We know something of the gradual process by which the church was built. We see the arches and windows as solutions to technical problems as well as objects of beauty. Perhaps we have begun to learn the iconography, the process of interpretation by which anonymous statues of apparently similar angels and saints turn into Bible stories. Understanding the groups of statuary over a doorway is very like deciphering a picture by Picasso. We say: "Ah, of course, that must be Saint Stephen," just as after studying a Picasso for a while we may say: "Of course, there is her elbow, sticking out of her head."

But we are left with more questions.

Readers sometimes ask: How do you know so much about the medieval builders? Some of our information comes from pictures. When medieval artists made illustrations for Bibles they often depicted the tower of Babel. The story, in the book of Genesis, is that men decided to build a tower up to heaven, and their arrogance displeased

God, who made them all speak different languages, so that in the resulting confusion the project was abandoned. Those illustrations, showing stone masons and mortar makers, scaffolding, and hoists, give us a lot of evidence about medieval building sites.

Other sources of information about cathedral builders include surviving contracts between the chapter and the builders, for example, and payroll records. One of the books that inspired me to write *The Pillars of the Earth* is *The Cathedral Builders (Les bâtisseurs de cathédrales)* by Jean Gimpel, whom I mentioned earlier. When I began work on *Pillars* I decided to get in touch with Gimpel to ask him to be a historical consultant for my novel. I knew that the Gimpels were a famous French family of art dealers and I assumed he would live in Paris. However, not only did he live in London but on my street. He agreed to be one of my consultants for *Pillars,* and all he asked in payment was a case of champagne. We became friends and table-tennis opponents, and he beat me every week.

When I began *Pillars,* in January 1986, I wanted to understand, for myself, and to explain, for readers, how and why the medieval cathedrals were built, and why they look the way they do. I hope *Pillars* shows how the construction

of a cathedral served the different interests of each major power group in medieval society: monarchy, aristocracy, priesthood, traders, townspeople, and peasants.

In March of 1989 I wrote "The End" on the last page of *The Pillars of the Earth*. It had taken me three years and three months to write, but I had been thinking about it much longer.

I was not the first author to be inspired by cathedrals. Victor Hugo is the greatest, to my mind. Anthony Trollope made the fictional Barchester Cathedral the center of a six-novel series, *The Chronicles of Barsetshire*. William Golding won the Nobel Prize for an oeuvre that included *The Spire,* a dizzying story of a priest's obsession with building a four-hundred-foot spire on top of a cathedral that has no proper foundations. T. S. Eliot wrote a verse play, *Murder in the Cathedral*, about the assassination in 1170 of Thomas Becket, the archbishop of Canterbury. Raymond Carver wrote a story called "Cathedral" about a blind man drawing a cathedral, and Nelson DeMille wrote a thriller, also called *Cathedral*, about the IRA taking over St. Patrick's Cathedral on Fifth Avenue in New York.

Each of us was enraptured by something different. I

saw the building of the cathedral as the kind of communal enterprise that captures the imagination of an entire society. A cathedral is a work of art, but it was never the brainchild of one person. Although there was always a master mason who drew the basic designs, he relied for the detailed work on a small army of artists and craftsmen, all of whom had their own talents and used their own imaginations. In some ways he was like the producer of a movie, who manages actors, writers, set designers, costume makers, makeup artists, and lighting specialists, and tries to get each of them to give the best of what his or her genius has to offer. For me, the cathedral is about what people can achieve when they work together.

Furthermore, this work of art could not be made unless thousands more people supported the project. It was the achievement of an entire community. In *Pillars* I wrote about how the building of the cathedral drew in people from every sector of medieval society: not just the clergy but also aristocrats, businesspeople, city dwellers, and rural agriculturalists. They gave support and money, a lot of money. Everyone benefited. Employment was created, commerce was strengthened, markets grew up,

international migration was stimulated, and new technology was constantly being invented and spread. In my novel those who oppose the building do so only because they want it built somewhere else.

I have compared the building of a cathedral to a space launch. It involved the whole of society in the same way; it developed cutting-edge technology; it brought widespread economic benefits—and yet when you add up all the pragmatic reasons, they're not quite enough to explain why we did it. There is another element, which is the spiritual, the human being's need to aspire to something above the material life. When you've seen how each group in Kingsbridge serves its own interest, you haven't yet grasped the full picture. *Pillars* also explains that it was also done for the glory of God.

Not long ago I was on the roof of Peterborough Cathedral. Some of the pinnacles had been replaced in the 1950s, and I noticed that the new ones were crude, lacking detail, by comparison with the highly decorated medieval features beside them. The difference was not visible from the ground, and evidently the craftsmen of the 1950s thought there was no point in carving details that no one

could see. The medieval builders would have disagreed. They made the unseen parts just as carefully as those on public view because, after all, God could see them.

A journalist asked me: "Don't you hate all the tourists in their shorts with their cameras?" No. Cathedrals have always been full of tourists. In the Middle Ages they were not called tourists, they were pilgrims, but they traveled for many of the same reasons: to see the world and its marvels, to broaden their minds, to educate themselves, and perhaps to come in touch with something miraculous, otherworldly, eternal.

I believe that a novel is successful to the extent that it touches the emotions of the reader. And something similar may be true of all works of art. It is certainly true of cathedrals. Our encounters with them are emotional. When we see them we are awestruck. When we walk around we are enraptured by their grace and light. When we sit quietly we are possessed by a sense of peace.

And when one burns, we weep.

Written between April 19 and 26, 2019,
in Knebworth, England.

ACKNOWLEDGMENTS

The first draft of this essay was read and helpfully criticized by John Clare, Barbara Follett, and l'equipe française—Cecile Boyer-Runge, Clare Do-Serro, Maggie Doyle, and Marine Alata at Éditions Robert Laffont. I am grateful to them all.

ART CREDITS

Insert page 1 top: Saint évêque, c. 1425 de Fra Angelico, église San Domenico, Fiesole, Italie © Metropolitan Museum of Art, New York, USA/Bridgeman Images; page 1 bottom: © AKG Images/ De Agostini/Biblioteca Ambrosiana; page 2: La liberté guidant le peuple, 28 juillet 1830, c.1830-31 d'Eugène Delacroix © Louvre-Lens, France/Bridgeman Images; page 3 left: © Carole Rabourdin/Bibliothèque de la maison de Victor Hugo/Roger-Viollet; page 3 right: © Franck/Tallandier/Bridgeman Images; page 4: collection particulière; page 5: © Museum of the History of Science, Broad Street, Oxford, England; page 6: collection particulière; page 7 top: © Musée Carnavalet/Roger-Viollet; page 7 bottom: © Granger/Bridgeman Images; page 8 top: The Imperial War Museums collection; page 8 bottom: © Program33 / France.TV / "The secrets of the builders: Notre-Dame" by Emmanuel Blanchard.

COMING IN FALL 2020

the long-awaited prequel to
The Pillars of the Earth

The Evening and the Morning

by Ken Follett